Kids have an innate curiosity about how their bodies work. The human body is indeed a fascinating subject, and after all, nothing is closer to us than our own selves. Surprisingly, many of us, parents and kids included, don't understand much about how our bodies work.

Naturopathic doctor Heather Manley experienced firsthand students' bright-eyed excitement for learning about the human body when she volunteered to share her medical knowledge with her young kids' schoolmates. Dr. Manley realized that human anatomy and physiology can be made accessible at any age, provided it's presented in the right way. Not finding just the right teaching materials out there, Dr. Manley set out to create them herself with the Human Body Detectives series, which takes kids on journeys through body systems as if the body is a magical kingdom packed with adventure, which in many ways it really is.

Learning about our bodies not only ignites an interest in science, but is also a powerful tool for teaching kids how to stay healthy and prevent disease. Human Body Detectives instills the basic principles of a healthy lifestyle along the way—eat well, be active, get enough sleep and be socially engaged—in a most pleasurable way.

Enjoy the journey!

Ayala Laufer-Cahana M.D.
Pediatrician, artist, mom, and founder of Herbal Water Inc.

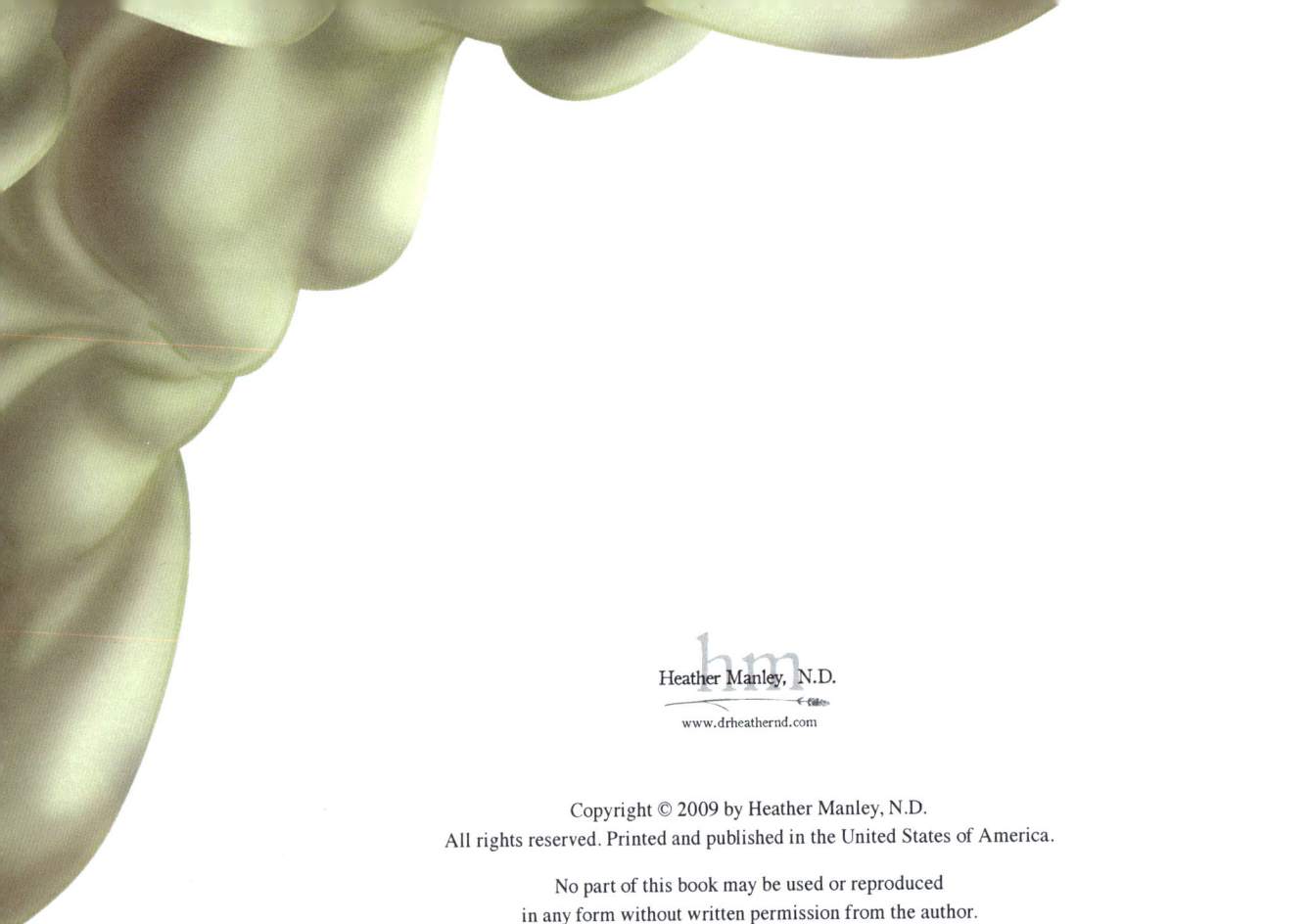

Heather Manley, N.D.
www.drheathernd.com

Copyright © 2009 by Heather Manley, N.D.
All rights reserved. Printed and published in the United States of America.

No part of this book may be used or reproduced
in any form without written permission from the author.

For reproduction of any part of this book or for more information please contact:
Heather Manley, N.D. | e: drheather@drheathernd.com | www.drheathernd.com | www.humanbodydetectives.com

human body detectives

A Heart Pumping Adventure

CASE FILE #3

Dr. Heather Manley

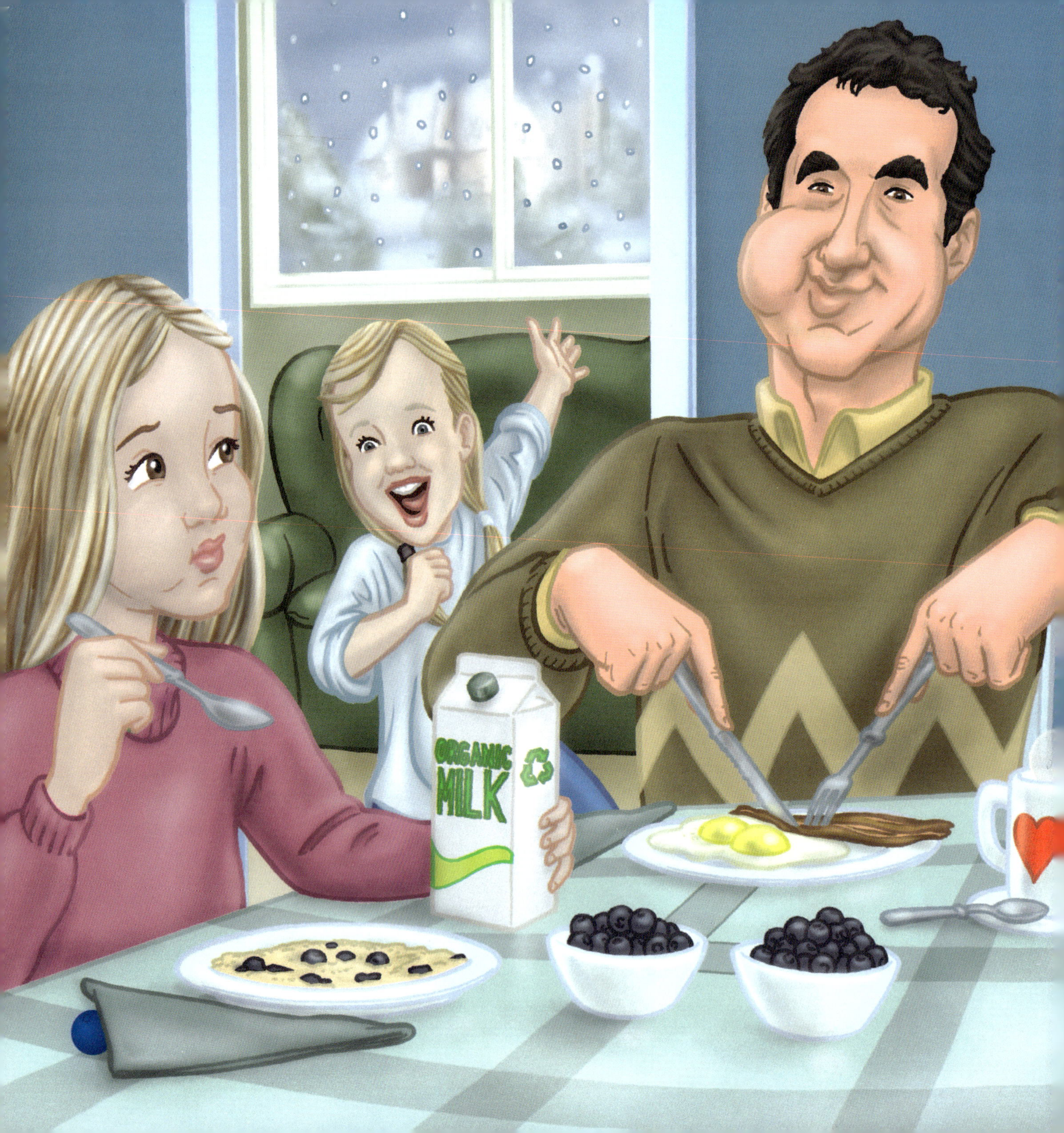
ORGANIC
MILK

It was a dark, snowy morning and Merrin wanted to stay cozy under her covers, but she managed to STUMBLE out of bed and into the kitchen for breakfast. As she ate her hot oatmeal with organic blueberries and milk, she saw her dad drinking coffee and happily overindulging in his daily bacon and fried eggs. She had just been reading about the circulatory system for school and knew that her dad was eating a lot of unhealthy fat, which could damage his ♥. Then Pearl came storming into the kitchen and interrupted Merrin's worried thoughts with her big, loud voice.

"MERRIN, LETS GO OUTSIDE, IT'S A PERFECT DAY FOR TOBOGGANING OR ICE SKATING!"

"Let me have breakfast first and then I want to finish my book on the circulatory system."

"The *WHAT* system?" Pearl asked.

Merrin, ignoring her sister and rolling her eyes, finished her last bite of breakfast then moved to the sofa to settle in with her book. Pearl listened as Merrin read out loud.

♥ =heart

"'The circulatory system is made up of the heart, the blood and the blood vessels. The blood vessels are like tubes that carry the blood in a big circle around the body. The heart beats 100,000 times a day to push the blood to all parts of the body.' Wow! So it must deliver oxygen and nutrients throughout the body."

"Oh," Pearl said and added, "Hey, I know a way to make this book a little more exciting."

"I don't think that's a good idea, Pearl. You remember what happened last time?"

"Yeah, I do, and *IT WAS FUN!* Maybe we need to do some human body detective work.

"Well, I did see Dad eating a very unhealthy breakfast."

"Okay, then let's go look inside Dad's circulatory system. Where's your book?"

Merrin hesitated, but then grabbed her book. The sisters squeezed their eyes shut and visualized themselves in their dad's ♥. Pearl smiled as the DIZZINESS settled in. She knew the magic was starting...

When the DIZZY, swirling feeling stopped, Pearl was the first to open her eyes and look around. "Hmmm," she muttered as she looked down and saw she was sitting on a red, pillowy donut-shaped thing, and floating on a red-colored sea.

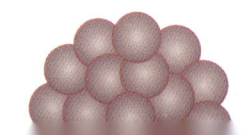

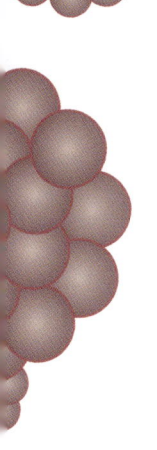

Now realizing what she had asked for, Pearl cried frantically, "What are we on?"

Merrin took a deep breath and looked around. All she could see were a bunch of green grape-like things. *Weird*, she thought, *I thought we were going to the heart*. But then it came to her. "Ohhh, we're on a red blood cell, or erythrocyte! It travels around the body delivering and picking up oxygen and carbon dioxide. Not sure what those grape-like things are, though."

"You mean we're going to ride this red blood cell like a toboggan around the body? And all this red stuff sure isn't snow! Let's get out of here!" Pearl could feel her own ♥ pumping hard.

"Gosh, Pearl. You were the one who wanted this, so we're going for the ride. What does Mom call that? A consequence? And remember, we're here to help Dad."

"All right, but what IS all this red-colored water?" Pearl asked in a whiny voice.

"I think it's blood," Merrin answered casually.

"What! We're floating around on BLOOD? That's disgusting!"

"Duh, we're in the body. What did you expect?"

Wait a minute, Merrin thought, remembering a picture of those grape-like things in her book. "Hey, we're in the lungs and those are alveoli."

"HEY THAT SOUNDS LIKE RAVIOLI!"

"Yeah, you're right. But they're where the red blood cells will pick up oxygen."

"So we're in the lungs floating on a red blood cell whose job it is to deliver oxygen?" Pearl asked.

"Yeah, and also to get rid of carbon dioxide. Hey, look at the other red blood cells ahead of us. Something is jumping on and off of them. It must be oxygen and well, the carbon dioxide."

"I know oxygen is the air we breathe, but what's carbon dioxide? Will it hurt us?

"Nah, it's a gas that the body is trying to get rid of," Merrin said. "It leaves the lungs when you breath out or exhale."

As they quickly approached the alveoli, their donut-shaped boat began to wobble.

Pearl started to panic and squeezed her eyes shut. This made her lose her balance and she began to fall overboard. Head first!

"MERRIN! I'M FALLING!"

5

Merrin anxiously turned to Pearl and reached out to grab her legs, but they were wet and slippery. She wasn't sure she could hold on. She gripped tighter, but still her hands slipped. Then luckily, at the last moment, she was able to grip Pearl's ankles. She quickly pulled her in.

"That was close, Pearl. Be more careful!"

Merrin and Pearl turned and watched in amazement as carbon dioxide jumped off their dark reddish blood cell and oxygen jumped on.

"Wow, look how Squishy has changed color. She's like a bright red apple," Pearl observed.

"Squishy?"

"Yup, Squishy, our red blood cell," said Pearl, giving the red blood cell a pat.

"Red blood cells with oxygen are bright red, whereas red blood cells with carbon dioxide are a dull, dark red color," Merrin explained. "Squishy is now full of oxygen."

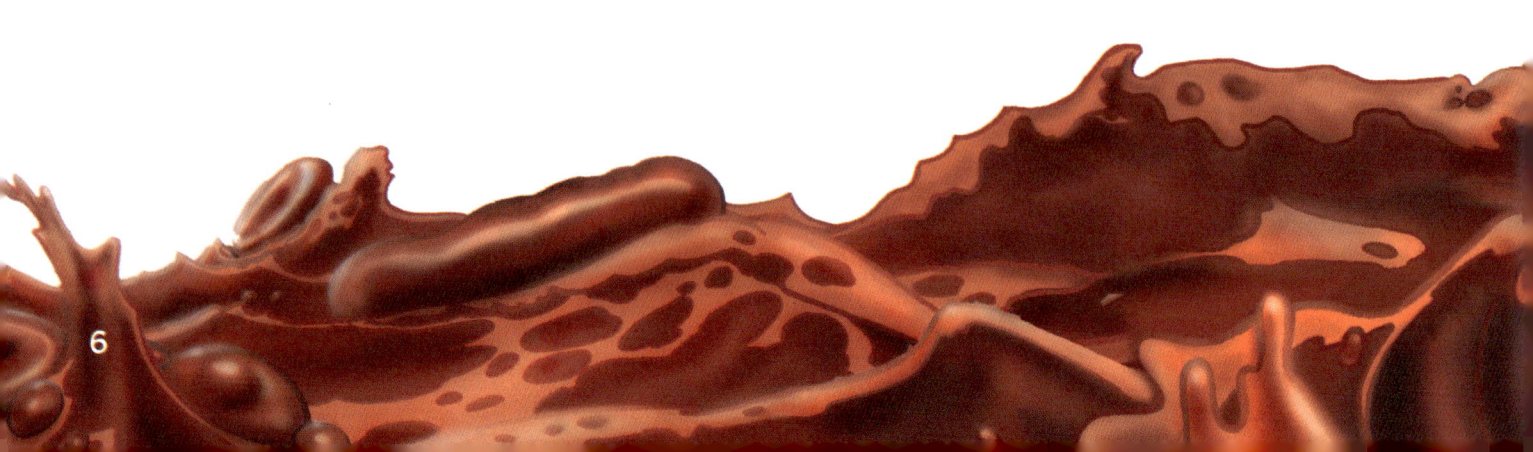

"The first organ to receive oxygen is the heart. So we must be headed to the heart." Then sooner than Pearl expected, Merrin exclaimed, "I see the four different chambers of the heart!"

"What do you mean, four chambers?" Pearl questioned.

"Well, the heart has four chambers, like four different rooms, called ventricles and atria. The left and right atria receive blood from the lungs and then dump the blood into the ventricles, then the ventricles send the blood to the rest of the body. Got it?" Merrin asked. But Pearl was fixated on something else.

"Ewww!" Pearl exclaimed, noticing yellowish, gooey stuff on the walls of the blood vessel.

Right then, Squishy lodged itself in the goo. Merrin, being as brave as she could, reached out her hand and gave a big push off the sticky blood vessel wall. But they didn't budge.

Pearl desperately wanted to get unstuck. A thought came to her, then she said, "What if we push off with our legs?"

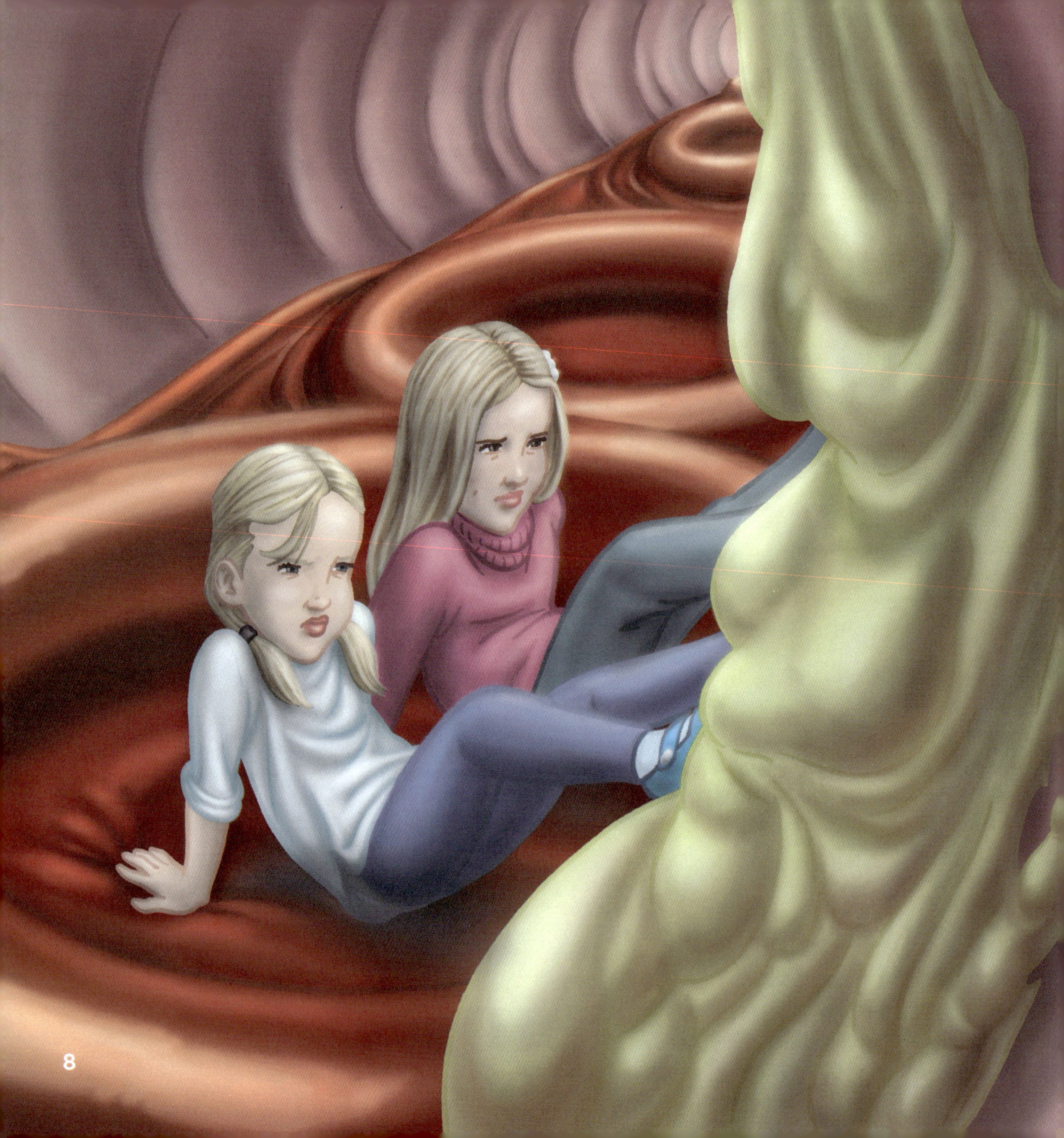

So, sitting on Squishy, using all their leg strength, they counted, "1-2-3!" and pushed. It was not so easy. Merrin fell safely back on Squishy, but Pearl's legs were knee high in the yellow goop. She was lodged so firmly that Merrin did not know how she would pull her out. She decided to grab her by the waist and yank with all her might. Pearl came flying away. Free at last!

"That was disgusting," Merrin exclaimed.

"BEYOND DISGUSTING. LOOK AT MY SHOES!"

Then they heard a familiar voice, sounding echo-y and far away.

"What's that feeling?" said their Dad. "It feels like someone is poking me inside."

Both girls looked at each other and began to giggle.

"Hey, honey, it feels like someone is tickling inside my heart! Am I ok?" their Dad asked their Mom.

"Oh, I'm sure you're fine," their mom replied. "But maybe you shouldn't eat so much bacon and fried eggs. Not so heart healthy. You might want to get back running on that treadmill, too."

"You're right. I know. I know," they heard their dad complain.

Merrin remembered that gooey, sticky stuff. "My book mentioned that the heart's blood vessels sometimes get a buildup of fat that can restrict blood flow to the heart."

"Restrict? Do you mean that the heart will not get the nutrients it needs? Remember what we learned in the digestive system? How the blood carries nutrients from food to feed the body? We better tell Dad."

"Well, I know there are good fats and bad fats. Bad fats are in greasy foods like potato chips and french fries, and good fats come from fish and nuts," Merrin continued. "The heart also likes the nutrient magnesium, which is in things like beans and spinach and helps the heart muscle relax. And fiber—like in oatmeal, fruits and vegetables—which grabs onto stuff the body doesn't want and well, poops it out so it doesn't stick to the blood vessel walls."

"Nice... I guess Dad needs more fiber to get rid of that yellow gooey stuff in his blood vessels. Our mission will be to have him eat fruits, vegetables, nuts and seeds... I love apples and almonds, so I guess my heart does, too!" Pearl added.

"I wonder where we're going now," Merrin said.

"I bet to the liver to pick up some nutrients. Remember you said that the blood is the delivery system of the body?" Pearl said. "And I remember from our first adventure that the liver stores the nutrients."

"Good thinking, Pearl! Look ahead. I see something. It must be the liver!"

Merrin and Pearl floated down towards the liver. As they entered the liver, they saw the oxygen jumping off Squishy.

SPLASH!

Merrin looked behind her and saw wave ripples in the blood. She saw Pearl climbing onto another red blood cell.

Merrin screamed, "WHAT ARE YOU DOING?"

"SOMETHING PUSHED ME OFF!" Pearl explained.

"JUMP BACK!"

They were drifting further and further apart. Pearl looked at her sister like she was crazy. There was no way she could jump that far! But the longer she waited, the wider the gap became. Merrin was frantic and Pearl was scared.

Then suddenly, a yellow FLASH and a friendly, smiley face appeared before them.

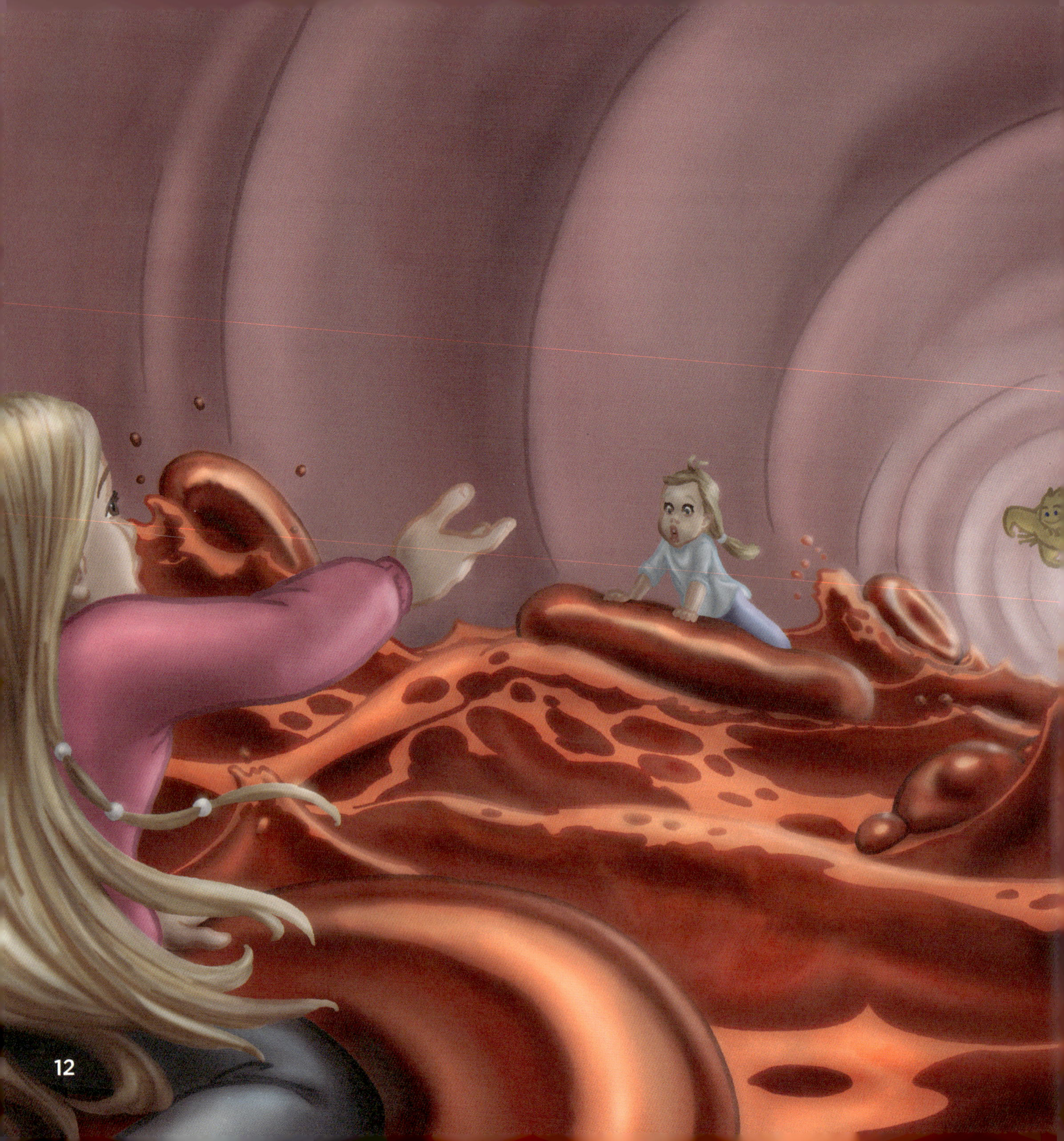

"**QUICKSTER!**" Pearl yelled, recognizing the friendly white blood cell whom they had helped in their last adventure through the immune system!

"Hi. I'm Quickster's grandson, **SPEEDY**," the white blood cell replied. Merrin didn't want to say anything, but she did remember reading about the short lifespan of white blood cells. She felt a bit sad and missed Quickster.

SPEEDY continued, "Gramps told me all about you guys and the great work you do. I'm happy to be at your service today." He gestured for Pearl to jump on his back. She did so gladly and **SPEEDY** swiftly returned her to Merrin and Squishy.

"That was sure lucky," Merrin said with a grateful sigh of relief, as Pearl leapt onto Squishy. The girls blew **SPEEDY** kisses of heartfelt thanks as he zipped away.

Now it was obvious how dark Squishy was becoming. She was low on oxygen so they needed to head back to the lungs soon.

Merrin said, "Maybe some carbon dioxide jumped on and knocked you over!"

"Then I would have to say carbon dioxide is a little dangerous!" Pearl said, laughing.

"Yeah, I guess... Hey, I think we may go to the kidney next."

But wait, which one? There are two kidneys, one on each side of the body. Oh, I guess it doesn't matter which, Merrin thought.

"**LOOK AHEAD!**" Pearl screamed. "I see something that looks like those beans mom puts in our chili!"

"Merrin laughed. "You mean kidney beans? That's got to be the kidney."

"Well, what does the kidney do?"

"It cleans the blood so the body can get rid of the liquid waste the body doesn't need. It does this through urine."

"What's urine?" Pearl asked.

"Pearl, it's pee!" Merrin explained.

Pearl began to panic, "Oh, no! We're not going to get peed out of here, are we?"

"No, we have to go back to the lungs to drop off the carbon dioxide."

"Phew! Then I think we'd better get home," said Pearl.

The sisters sat comfortably on Squishy, their cushiony red blood cell boat, as they traveled back to the 🫀.

"Look, there it is!" exclaimed Pearl excitedly. "Which chamber will we go through? Hey what is that?" Pearl was pointing to an arch type thing on top of the 🫀.

"Ohhh, that is the arch of the aorta. It's the largest artery in the body.

The blood vessels are broken up into two groups—arteries and veins. The arteries carry blood away from the heart and the veins carry blood to the heart. Back to the right atrium we go!"

Merrin assumed correctly. As they went up and down and around the 🫀, they soon jetted out through the ventricles, and traveled back to the lungs to dump off the carbon dioxide.

"Look! It's those grape-like things again, Merrin!"

"Oh, yeah. I see the alveoli, too. We went through the whole body. We delivered all of the oxygen and now it's time to pick up some more. Do you want to do it all over again, Pearl?" Merrin teased her sister.

"ARE YOU KIDDING? I WANT TO GO TOBOGGANING! ON SNOW!" Pearl exclaimed.

Suddenly, Squishy began to move really fast. What was going on?

"Hold on, Pearl! Dad must be moving around or maybe even exercising! That will make the heart pump faster to get the oxygen to all the muscles..."

Pearl grabbed Merrin, but in doing so, caused them to lose their balance.

"AHHHHH!" they screamed as they fell towards the blood.

Pearl was safe, but Merrin hit Squishy and immediately plunged into the deep river of blood. The blood was moving faster than the red blood cells and Merrin soon disappeared from Pearl's sight.

Pearl could see Merrin's blonde hair bobbing away from her. What was she going to do! She realized her only choice was to carefully jump from one red blood cell to another until she caught up to her sister. She said a sad goodbye to Squishy and was off. The first few leaps were shaky but then she got into a rhythm and soon enough she could see Merrin climbing onto a red blood cell in front of her.

"MERRIN, I'M RIGHT HERE!"

Merrin, wiping nervous sweat from her forehead, turned around, looking extremely relieved to see her sister.

Pearl said, "Gosh, where was **SPEEDY** when we needed him that time?"

"Probably off looking for bad bugs in the immune system somewhere. But you know, I think we're getting pretty good at this human body detective thing. I bet he knew we could do it!" said Merrin reassuringly. "C'mon. We've got to get back to warn Dad about his heart. Here, take my hands."

They closed their eyes and envisioned their dad eating a healthy dinner of wild salmon, green beans and brown rice. They also saw his pumping strongly. They felt that DIZZY, swirling sensation come on strong. As soon as it stopped and all felt calm, they blinked their eyes open to find themselves sitting, all cozy, at home on their sofa.

"Phew, we're back," Merrin said gratefully.

Their dad walked in at that moment, kind of sweaty, wearing a t-shirt and shorts and a towel around his neck. "**HEY, GIRLS!**" he said. "Your mom encouraged me to run on the treadmill for a bit. Said it's good for my heart. But now I've worked up a big appetite for lunch. What do you say we go out for hamburgers and fries?"

Merrin and Pearl shook their heads, thinking the same thing. All they could think of was that **yellow goopy stuff** in his **blood** vessels...

"We have a better idea, Dad," announced Pearl.

Merrin chimed in, "Yeah, how about we stay here and make a nice, big colorful salad filled with veggies, nuts and seeds, instead!"

human body detectives

case solved

CASE FILE #3

How good of a detective are you?

Can you find...

and sneaky blueberry guy!

Let us know how many times you spotted each one at merrin@drheathernd.com or pearl@drheathernd.com

More About the Circulatory System

The **circulatory system** is made up of the **heart**, **blood vessels** and the **blood**. The heart is a powerful muscle, acting much like a pump that pushes blood throughout the body by way of the blood vessels, which are like long, thin, flexible tubes— similar to garden hoses. The blood carries nutrients and **oxygen** to all the organs and cells of your body, then picks up **carbon dioxide** and delivers it to the lungs to be breathed out. You might say that the circulatory system is your body's delivery system!

The heart is divided into four chambers. The top part of the heart holds the left atrium and the right atrium (together they are called **atria**). Below the atria are the two other chambers, the right and left **ventricles**. The atria fill with blood as

I ♥ HBD

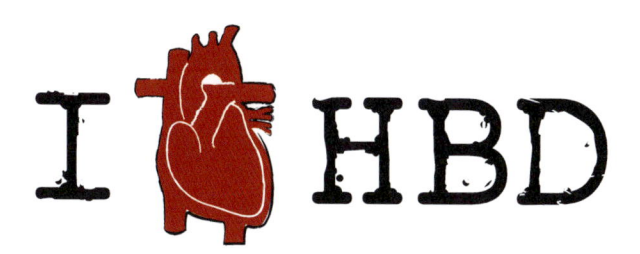

it returns to the heart then push the blood into the right and left ventricles. The ventricles then squeeze and contract to push the blood throughout the body. While the ventricles do that, the atria fill up with new blood again.

There are 4 valves that help regulate the blood going into the chambers of the heart. The mitral valve and the tricuspid valve let blood flow from the atria to the ventricles, and the aortic and pulmonary valves control the flow of the blood as it leaves the heart. All these valves make sure the blood moves forward and not backward. When the blood leaves the aortic and pulmonary valves, it travels through the blood vessels known as arteries, to all parts of the body. Veins, another type of blood vessel, take blood back to the heart.

Making up most of the blood that travels through the blood vessels are red blood cells, or **erythrocytes**. Red blood cells are made in the bone marrow, and their main job is to deliver oxygen throughout the body. The red blood cells will also pick up carbon dioxide, a gas formed by the body but not used, and take it back to the lungs to be breathed out. Red blood cells have a short but exciting and adventurous life. It takes a red blood cell about 20 seconds to travel around the whole body! They live approximately 100 to 120 days, and in a healthy adult, 2 million new red blood cells are made per second.

The heart pumps away 24 hours a day, 7 days a week to keep the circulatory system working! The process never stops. When you feel your **heart beat**, that is your **pulse**. How many times per minute your heart beats is your heart rate. Your heart rate changes depending on the amount of activity you are doing. With each heart beat you feel, now you can picture how your heart and the whole circulatory system work to keep your body strong, nourished and healthy!

The Heart

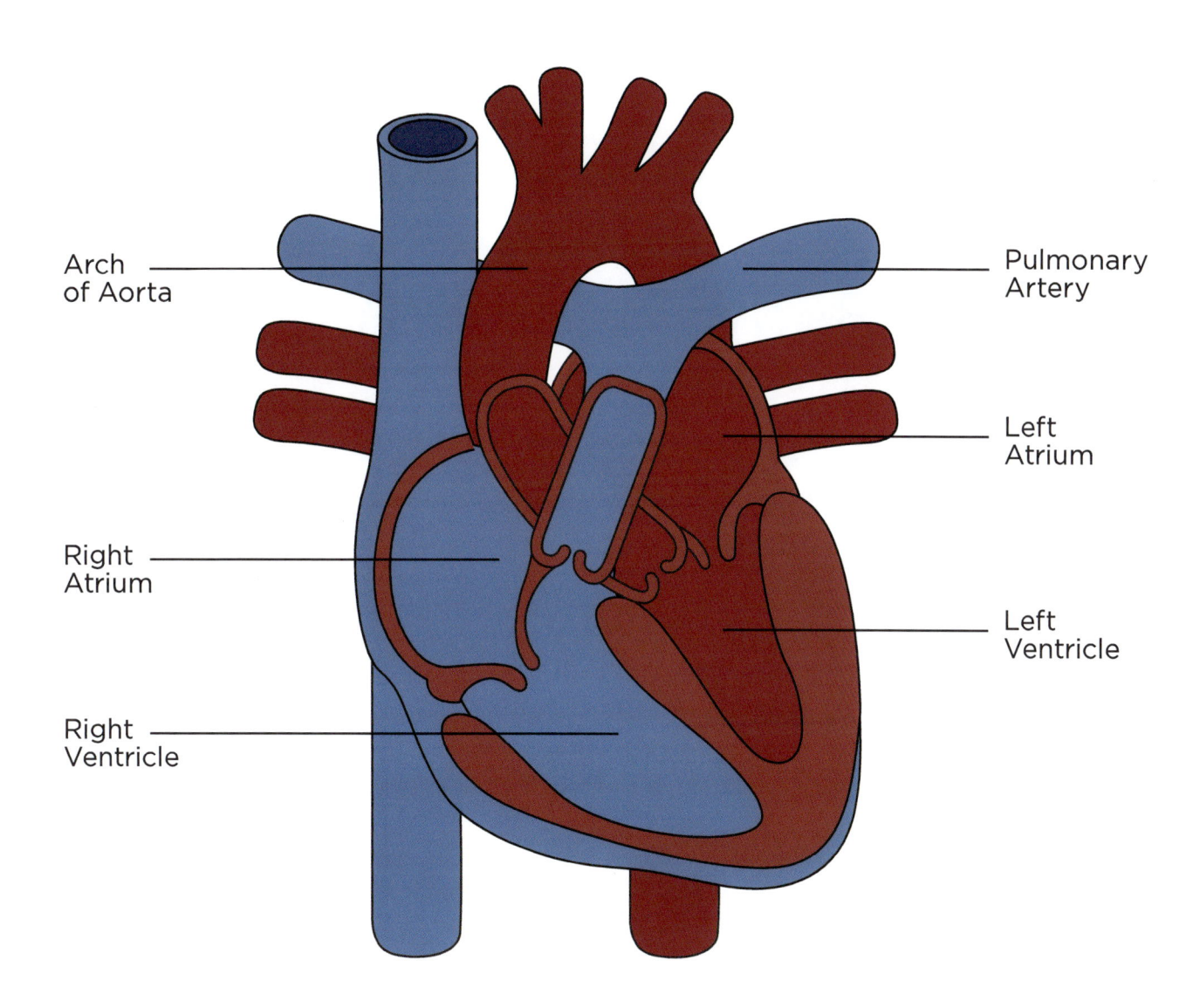

- Arch of Aorta
- Right Atrium
- Right Ventricle
- Pulmonary Artery
- Left Atrium
- Left Ventricle

Human Body Detectives Ask You...

These facts were news to Merrin, Pearl and Sam, so they wanted to share them with you.

did you know that...

- the heart contracts more than 100,000 times a day to push blood through about 60,000 miles (or 96,000 kilometers) of blood vessels?

- the average heart will pump approximately 1,800 gallons (or 6,800 liters) of blood each day?

- exercising will increase that number to as much as 6 times (that is 10,800 gallons & 40,800 liters)?

- the left ventricle has the hardest job of pushing the blood to the head and body? So it is super duper strong!

- you cannot make your heart stop or start? It works 24 hours a day, 7 days a week–that means all the time!

- each heartbeat is called a 'heart cycle'?

- when the blood travels to the lungs, it is called 'pulmonary circulation'?

- a healthy heart is about the same size as a pear?

- the heart is a muscle and needs exercise too?

- it takes about 60 seconds for the blood to pump to every part of your body?

- you can check your heart rate by pressing your index, second, and third fingers on the inside of your wrist?

- a heart doctor is called a cardiologist?

- the symbol for carbon dioxide is CO_2?

- the symbol for oxygen is O_2?

- your heart beats approximately 30 million times a year?

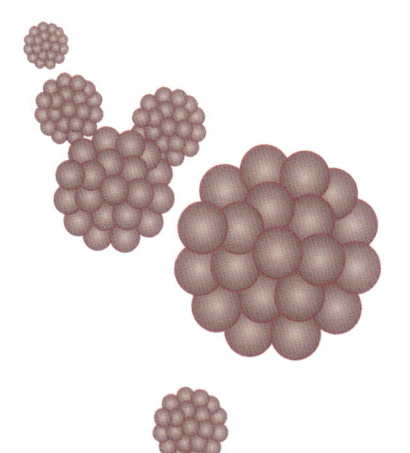

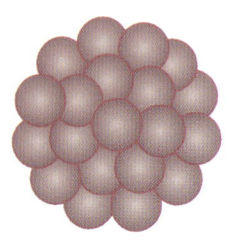

Merrin and Pearl Wonder...

The HBDs love foods rich in fiber. Fiber is an important part of food that grabs on to the not so healthy stuff in your body and moves it out as waste. People often think that fiber is good just for the digestive system, but it is also very important for your heart and circulatory system. As fiber moves through your digestive system, tiny particles of it get absorbed into your blood stream (remember this from HBD: *The Lucky Escape?*) and help keep your blood vessels clean, too!

Merrin and Pearl suggest three ways for you to boost your diet with **FIBER-PACKED** foods:

1. **Eat whole fruits and vegetables.** That means eating the peels, too. The peels on such foods as apples and cucumbers are rich sources of fiber.

2. **Be beany.** Almost all varieties of beans provide lots of fiber. Two of Merrin's and Pearl's favorites are kidney beans (usually found in chili) and garbanzo beans (also called chickpeas). Garbanzo beans are especially yummy when made into hummus, a delicious dip for carrots, cucumbers or crackers.

3. **Get nutty and nibble some seeds.** Add pumpkin, sunflower, flax, chia, or hemp seeds and your favorite nuts to your salads or vegetable dishes (broccoli and cashews taste great together!). They add not only fiber, but great taste and extra vitamins and minerals, too.

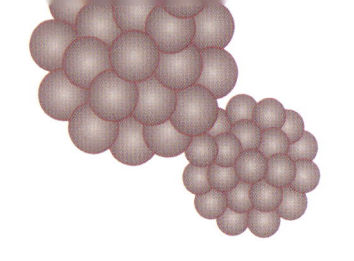

Laugh Your Heart Out

Human Body Detectives love a great case, and a funny joke! Remember what we learned in *Battle with the Bugs*? Laughing lowers levels of stress and strengthens the immune system. So go ahead, laugh loud and hard!

Why is the artichoke the most loving vegetable?
Because it has a heart!

Why did the banana go out with the prune?
Because he couldn't get a date!

What kind of flower do you have between your nose and chin?
Two lips!

What kind of flowers do you never give on Valentine's Day?
Cauliflowers!

Knock knock
Who's there?
Howard
Howard who?
Howard you like a big kiss?

What do you call cheese that is not your own?
Nacho cheese!

What do you get when you have 524 blueberries trying to get through the same door?
A blueberry jam

What is the kindest vegetable?
A sweet potato!

Knock knock
Who's there?
Pooch
Pooch who?
Pooch your arms around me, baby!

Your Pulse

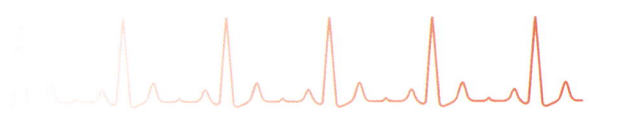

Merrin and Pearl love to check their pulse. Your pulse is your heart rate or the number of times your heart beats in one minute. Be a detective and see how your heart rate changes before and right after you exercise! You might want an adult to help you at first.

How to take your pulse:

1. Place the tips of your index, second, and third fingers on the palm side of your opposite wrist, directly below the base of your thumb.

2. Press lightly with your fingers until you feel the blood pulsing beneath your fingers. You may need to move your fingers around until you feel it.

3. Use a watch or a clock with a second hand.

4. Count the beats you feel for 10 seconds. Multiply this number by six to get your heart rate or pulse per minute.

Check your pulse while resting: _____ x 6 = _____
(before exercising)   (beats in 10 seconds)   (your pulse)

Check your pulse right after exercising: _____ x 6 = _____
                               (beats in 10 seconds)   (your pulse)

Glossary

A list of useful circulatory words and their meaning.

Alveoli (AL-vee-oh-lye) Alveoli are located in the lungs and are the site of the primary gas exchange of oxygen and carbon dioxide.

Blood (BLUD) Blood is a body fluid that delivers nutrients and oxygen throughout the body, and transports waste or carbon dioxide to the lungs to be exhaled.

Blood vessels (BLUD VES-sels) The blood vessels are like long, thin tubes that transport blood throughout the body. There are two major types of blood vessels: arteries, which carry the blood away from the heart; and veins, which carry blood from the capillaries back toward the heart.

Carbon dioxide (CO_2) (CAR-bohn dye-OX-ide) Like oxygen, it is a colorless, odorless gas. It is formed in the body as a waste product and humans breathe it out through their lungs.

Circulatory system (SIR-kyuh-la-tor-ee SIS-tem) The circulatory system is made up of blood, blood vessels (veins, arteries and capillaries), and the heart.

Heart (HART) The heart is really a very strong muscle. It's located a little to the left of the middle of your chest, and is about the size of your fist. The heart pumps to send blood throughout your body. The blood supplies your body with the oxygen and nutrients it needs and also carries away waste.

Heart rate/pulse (HART RATE/PUHLS) Your pulse is your heart rate, or the number of times your heart beats per minute. Before each beat, the heart fills with blood. Then the heart muscle squeezes and pushes the blood out. Your heart does this constantly. When you feel your heart beat, that is your pulse.

Organ (OR-gahn) The kidney, liver, heart, stomach, and large intestine are all examples of organs in the human body. They have very specific and important functions to keep humans alive and well.

Oxygen (O_2) (OX-ih-jen) Oxygen is a colorless and odorless gas that humans breathe in and need to survive.

Red blood cell/erythrocyte (RED BLUD SEL/ehr-ITH-roh-site) Red blood cells, or erythrocytes, are red, donut–shaped cells found in the blood whose primary job is to deliver oxygen (O_2) throughout the body.

Ventricles and atria (VEN-trih-kuhls and AY-tree-ah) Humans have a four–chambered heart. Two of the chambers are called the right and left ventricles and the other two are called the left and right atria (singular=atrium). The ventricles pump blood out of the heart and the atria receives blood from the lungs.

Dr. Heather is a practicing naturopathic physician who promotes wellness and naturopathic healthcare on her website **drheathernd.com**. She is also the author of the award winning book series, *Human Body Detectives*. Dr. Heather lives on the Big Island of Hawaii with her husband and two daughters, and is currently at work on the next Human Body Detectives adventure.

tweet with Dr. Heather on Twitter: twitter.com/drheathernd

Audio versions and apps of all the **Human Body Detectives** books—*Battle with the Bugs, The Lucky Escape* and *A Heart Pumping Adventure*, are available on iTunes.

Visit the **Human Body Detectives** website for free downloads, to view the HBD book trailers, and to watch Human Body Detectives Merrin and Pearl in the kitchen and visiting exciting places!

visit us on Facebook: facebook.com/HumanBodyDetectives

LOOK FOR OTHER BOOKS IN THE HUMAN BODY DETECTIVE SERIES:
The Lucky Escape and *Battle with the Bugs*

kids are saying

"I liked listening to an adventure that happens inside the human body!"
Natalie, age 6

"It is so cool that Merrin and Pearl get to go on an adventure in the red sea!"
Aidan, age 7 and Sean, age 9

adults are saying

"The Human Body Detective stories teach children about their own bodies, health and well-being in a creative, engaging and lively way. The adventures are not only educational but suspenseful and humorous."
Susan, mom

"The series is a great way to help your children become more aware of their bodies and how the foods they eat can affect them."
babyvibe.ca

"Human Body Detectives is the perfect combination of entertainment and education. In fact, I doubt kids will realize just how much they're learning! I highly recommend it."
Greg Nigh, ND, Lac, Nature Cures Clinic

www.humanbodydetectives.com